GOD'S
BIG
INSTRUCTION
BOOK

RELATED TITLES PUBLISHED
BY ONEWORLD

Words to Comfort, Words to Heal

God's BIG Book of Virtues

GOD'S
BIG
INSTRUCTION
BOOK

*Timeless Wisdom on how to
Follow the Spiritual Path*

COMPILED BY JULIET MABEY

ONEWORLD

OXFORD

GOD'S BIG INSTRUCTION BOOK

Oneworld Publications
(Sales and Editorial)
185 Banbury Road
Oxford OX2 7AR
England

Oneworld Publications
(US Marketing Office)
160 N Washington St.
4th floor, Boston
MA 02114, USA

http://www.oneworld-publications.com

ISBN 1–85168–170–1

Cover and text design by Design Deluxe, Bath
Printed by CTPS, Hong Kong

CONTENTS

PERSONAL SPIRITUALITY

B ECAUSE THOU art greatly loved by Me, therefore
I shall tell thee what is good for thee.

HINDUISM: *Bhagavad Gita 18.64*

PREFACE

JUST AS the beauty of a garden lies in the diversity of its trees and flowers, so too the garden of the spirit derives its splendor and charm from the variety of its forms of expression. God's BIG Instruction Book draws on the words of wisdom from the diverse sacred scriptures of the world, humanity's common religious heritage. Together these spiritual fruits of the different world faiths have transformed the lives of people all over the world for thousands of years.

These simple verses were chosen for their timelessness, and for their ability to go beyond the religious traditions in which they are found. Here they explore the universal truths of the spiritual life, from the mystical relationship of the individual with God to those divine virtues that make us truly, fully human, such as love, honesty, and selflessness.

Spirituality should not be confused with religiosity or isolation from the hustle and bustle of everyday concerns, but rather is a way of living the everyday within the consciousness of the eternal. Indeed, it provides the very source of that quality, meaning, and purpose that makes our everyday life worthwhile. These inspirational words serve to remind us that a more fulfilling, complete life lies ahead for all who venture along the spiritual path.

JULIET MABEY

GOD

*God is in thy heart, yet thou searchest for Him
in the wilderness.*

SIKHISM: *Adi Granth*

OUR RELATIONSHIP
WITH GOD

OD HAS declared: I am close to the thought that My servant has of Me, and I am with him whenever he recollects Me. If he remembers Me in himself, I remember him in Myself, and if he remembers Me in a gathering I remember him better than those in the gathering do, and if he approaches Me by as much as one hand's length, I approach him by a cubit ... If he takes a step toward Me, I run toward him.

ISLAM: *Hadith*

EHOLD, I stand at the door and knock; if any one hears My voice and opens the door, I will come in to him and eat with him, and he with Me.

CHRISTIANITY: *Revelation 3.20*

T HE LORD lives in the heart of every creature. He turns them round and round upon the wheel of His Maya. Take refuge utterly in Him. By His grace you will find supreme peace, and the state which is beyond all change.

HINDUISM: *Bhagavad Gita 18.61–62*

N O MAN that seeketh Us will We ever disappoint, neither shall he that hath set his face towards Us be denied access unto Our court.

BAHÁ'Í FAITH: *Gleanings 126*

H E IS not far from each one of us, for "In Him we live and move and have our being."

CHRISTIANITY: *Acts 17.27–28*

THIS DO I ask, O Lord, reveal unto me the truth!
Who is the first begetter, father of the Cosmic Law?
Who assigned orbit to the sun and the stars?
Who causes the moon to wax and again to wane?
Who other than Thee? This and else I wish to know!

Who is the upholder of the earth and of the sky?
Who prevents them from falling down?
Who maintains the waters and also the plants?
Who yoked speed to winds and clouds?
Who is the creator of the creatures?

Who is the architect of light and darkness?
Who created sleep and wakefulness?
By whom exists down, midday and night,
Which monitor the duties of men?

ZOROASTRIANISM: *Avesta, Yasna 44.3–5*

A BIDE IN Me, and I in you. As the branch cannot bear fruit by itself, unless it abides in the vine, neither can you, unless you abide in Me.

I am the vine, you are the branches, He who abides in Me, and I in him, he it is that bears much fruit, for apart from Me you can do nothing. If a man does not abide in Me, he is cast forth as a branch and withers; and the branches are gathered, thrown into the fire and burned. If you abide in Me, and My words abide in you, ask whatever you will, and it shall be done for you. By this My Father is glorified, that you bear much fruit, and so prove to be My disciples. As the Father has loved Me, so have I loved you; abide in My love. If you keep My commandments, you will abide in My love, just as I have kept My Father's commandments and abide in His love. These things I have spoken to you, that My joy may be in you, and that your joy may be full.

CHRISTIANITY: *John 15.4–11*

TRUST IN the Lord with all your heart, and do not rely on your own insight. In all your ways acknowledge Him and He will make straight your paths.

JUDAISM: *Proverbs 3.5–6*

IN THE golden city of the heart dwells
The Lord of Love, without parts, without stain.
Know Him as the radiant light of light.
There shines not the sun, neither moon nor star,
Nor flash of lightning, nor fire lit on earth.
The Lord is the light reflected by all.
He shining, everything shines after Him.

HINDUISM: *Mundake Upanishad 2.2.10–11*

WE INDEED created man; and We know what his soul whispers within him, and We are nearer to him than the jugular vein.

ISLAM: *Qur'an 50.16*

TWO THINGS have I required of thee;
deny me them not before I die:
Remove far from me vanity and lies:
    give me neither poverty nor riches;
    feed me with food convenient for me:
Lest I be full, and deny thee,
    and say, "Who is the LORD?"
Or lest I be poor, and steal,
    and take the name of my God in vain.

JUDAISM: *Proverbs 30.7–9*

I AM THE nucleus of every creature, Arjuna; for without Me nothing can exist, neither animate nor inanimate . . . Wherever you find strength, or beauty, or spiritual power, you may be sure that these have sprung from a spark of My essence.

HINDUISM: *Bhagavad Gita 10.39–41*

GOD ASKS nothing of any soul save that which He has given it.

ISLAM: *Qur'an 65.7*

KNOWLEDGE OF GOD

MOSES SAID to God, "If I come to the people of Israel and say to them, 'The God of your fathers has sent me to you,' and they ask me, 'What is His name?' what shall I say to them?"

God said to Moses, "I Am Who I Am." And He said, "Say this to the people of Israel, 'I Am' has sent me to you."

JUDAISM: *Exodus 3.13–15*

To KNOW the eternal is called enlightenment.
Not to know the eternal is to act blindly to result in disaster.
He who knows the eternal is all-embracing.
Being all-embracing, he is impartial.
Being impartial, he is kingly [universal].
Being kingly, he is one with Nature.
Being one with Nature, he is in accord with Tao.
Being in accord with Tao, he is everlasting,
And is free from danger throughout his lifetime.

TAOISM: *Tao Te Ching 16*

GOD IS the Light of the heavens and the earth.
The parable of His Light
is as if there were a Niche,
and within it a Lamp;
the Lamp enclosed in Glass:
The Glass as it were a brilliant star:
Lit from a blessed Tree,
an olive neither of the East nor of the West,
whose oil is well-nigh luminous,
though fire scarce touched it.
Light upon Light!
God guides whom He will to His Light:
God sets forth parables for men, and God knows all things.

ISLAM: *Qur'an 24.35*

THE PURPOSE of God in creating man hath been,
and will ever be, to enable him to know his Creator
and attain His Presence.

BAHÁ'Í FAITH: *Gleanings 29*

NO VISION can grasp Him, but His grasp is over all vision; He is above all comprehension, yet is acquainted with all things.

ISLAM: Qur'an 6.103

THE INFINITE is the source of joy. There is no joy in the finite. Only in the Infinite is there joy. Ask to know the Infinite.

HINDUISM: Chandogya Upanishad 7.23

HAVE YOU considered the soil you till!
Do you yourselves sow it, or are We the Sowers?
Did We will, We would make it broken orts,
and you will remain bitterly jesting –
"We are debt-loaded;
nay, we have been robbed."

Have you considered the water you drink?
Did you send it down from the clouds, or did We send it?
Did We will, We would make it bitter; so why are you not
thankful?

Have you considered the fire you kindle?
Did you make its timber to grow, or did We make it?
We Ourselves made it for a reminder, and a boon to
the desert-dwellers.

ISLAM: *Qur'an 56.63–73*

LOVE OF GOD

TO LOVE is to know Me,
My innermost nature,
the truth that I am.

HINDUISM: *Bhagavad Gita 18.55*

HEAVEN AND earth contain Me not, but the heart of My faithful servant contains Me.

ISLAM: *Hadith of Suhrawardi*

MY SON, do not despise the Lord's discipline
or be weary of His reproof,
for the Lord reproves him whom He loves,
as a father the son in whom he delights.

JUDAISM: *Proverbs 3.11–12*

B ELOVED, LET us love one another: for love is of God; and
every one that loveth is born of God, and knoweth
God. He that loveth not knoweth not God;
for God is love.

CHRISTIANITY: *1 John 4.7–8*

THE WORLD is a garden,
The Lord its gardener,
Cherishing all, none neglected.

SIKHISM: *Adi Granth, Majh Ashtpadi M.3*

WE REJOICE in our sufferings, knowing that suffering produces endurance, and endurance produces character, and character produces hope, and hope does not disappoint us, because God's love has been poured into our hearts.

CHRISTIANITY: *Romans 5.3–5*

IN ANY way that men love Me in that same way they find My love.

HINDUISM: *Bhagavad Gita 4.11*

ALLAH THE Almighty has said, "O son of Adam, so long as you call upon Me and ask of Me, I shall forgive you for what you have done, and I shall not mind. O son of Adam, were your sins to reach the clouds of the sky and were you to then ask forgiveness of Me, I would forgive you. O son of Adam, were you to come to Me with sins nearly as great as the earth and were you to then face Me, ascribing no partner to Me, I would bring you forgiveness nearly as great as the earth."

ISLAM: *Forty Hadith of an-Nawawi 42*

"TEACHER, WHICH is the great commandment in the law?" Jesus said to him, "'You shall love the Lord your God with all your heart, and with all your soul, and with all your mind.' This is the great and first commandment. And the second is like it, 'You shall love your neighbor as yourself.' On these two commandments depend all the law and the prophets."

CHRISTIANITY: *Matthew 22.36–40*

SAY, O MY Servants who have transgressed against their souls! Despair not of the mercy of God: for God forgives all sins: for He is Oft-forgiving, Most Merciful.

ISLAM: *Qur'an 39.53*

Though a man be soiled with the sins of a lifetime, let him but love Me, rightly resolved, in utter devotion. I see no sinner, that man is holy.

Holiness soon shall refashion his nature to peace eternal. O son of Kunti, of this be certain: The man who loves Me shall not perish.

HINDUISM: *Bhagavad Gita 9.30–31*

O Son of Being! Love Me, that I may love thee. If thou lovest Me not, My love can in no wise reach thee.

BAHÁ'Í FAITH: *Arabic Hidden Words 5*

C OME TO Me, all who labor and are heavy laden, and I will give you rest. Take My yoke upon you, and learn from Me; for I am gentle and lowly in heart, and you will find rest for your souls. For My yoke is easy, and My burden is light.

CHRISTIANITY: *Matthew 11.28–30*

B E AWARE of Me always, adore Me, make every act an offering to Me, and you shall come to Me; this I promise, for you are dear to Me.

Abandon all supports and look to Me for protection. I shall purify you from the sins of the past; do not grieve.

HINDUISM: *Bhagavad Gita 18.65–66*

FEAR OF GOD

THE FEAR of the Lord is the beginning of wisdom.

JUDAISM: *Proverbs 9.10*

AND PETER opened his mouth and said, "Truly I perceive that God shows no partiality, but in every nation any one who fears Him and does what is right is acceptable to Him."

CHRISTIANITY: *Acts 10.34–35*

RELIGION IS a radiant light and an impregnable stronghold for the protection and welfare of the peoples of the world, for the fear of God impelleth man to hold fast to that which is good, and shun all evil.

BAHÁ'Í FAITH: *Tablets of Bahá'u'lláh*

IF YOU accept My words
and treasure My commandments;
If you make your ears attentive to wisdom
and your minds open to discernment;
If you call to understanding
and cry aloud to discernment,
If you seek it as you do silver
and search for it as for treasures,
Then you will understand the fear of the Lord
and attain Knowledge of God.

JUDAISM: *Proverbs 2.1–5*

GOD'S MESSENGERS

Whenever there is a decline in righteousness, O Bharat, and a rise in irreligion, then I send forth My Spirit.

For the Salvation of those who are good, for the destruction of evil in men, for the fulfillment of the kingdom of righteousness, I manifest Myself from age to age.

HINDUISM: *Bhagavad Gita 4.7–8*

And We have sent you to men as a Messenger; God suffices for a witness. Whosoever obeys the Messenger, thereby obeys God; and whosoever turns his back – We have not sent you to be a watcher over them.

ISLAM: *Qur'an 4.79–80*

Jesus spoke to them, saying, "I am the light of the world; he who follows Me will not walk in darkness, but will have the light of life."

CHRISTIANITY: *John 8.12*

V ERILY WE have raised in every nation a Messenger, proclaiming, "Serve God and shun false gods."

ISLAM: *Qur'an 16.36*

Y OU WILL know them by their fruits. Are grapes gathered from thorns, or figs from thistles? So, every sound tree bears good fruit, but the bad tree bears evil fruit. A sound tree cannot bear evil fruit, nor can a bad tree bear good fruit. Every tree that does not bear good fruit is cut down and thrown into the fire. Thus you will know them by their fruits.

CHRISTIANITY: *Matthew 7.16–20*

THEY SAID to him, "What must we do, to be doing the works of God?" Jesus answered them, "This is the work of God, that you believe in him whom He has sent."

CHRISTIANITY: *John 6.28–29*

THE PROPHETS and Messengers of God have been sent down for the sole purpose of guiding mankind to the straight Path of Truth. The purpose underlying their revelation hath been to educate all men, that they may, at the hour of death, ascend, in the utmost purity and sanctity and with absolute detachment, to the throne of the Most High.

BAHÁ'Í FAITH: *Gleanings 81*

THE PURPOSE OF LIFE

A religious man is guided in his activity not by the consequences of his action, but by the consciousness of the destination of his life.

Leo Tolstoy: Confessions

Following the Spiritual Path

T HIS IS true religion; to cleanse oneself with pure thoughts, pure words, and pure deeds.

ZOROASTRIANISM: *Zend Avesta*

I T IS you who must make the effort. The Great of the past only show the Way. Those who think and follow the path become free from the bondage of Mara . . .

A man should control his words and mind and should not do any harm with his body. If these ways of action are pure he can make progress on the path of the wise.

BUDDHISM: *Dhammapada 276, 281*

B Y SUSTAINED effort, earnestness, discipline, and self-control, let the wise man make for himself an island which no flood can overwhelm.

BUDDHISM: *Dhammapada 25*

I BEAR WITNESS, O my God, that Thou hast created me to know Thee and to worship Thee.

BAHÁ'Í FAITH: *Prayers and Meditations 181*

S EEK NOT for life on earth or in heaven. Thirst for life is delusion. Knowing life to be transitory, wake up from this dream of ignorance and strive to attain knowledge and freedom.

HINDUISM: *Srimad Bhagavatam 11.13*

TAKE AWAY from me the noise of your songs;
To the melody of your harps I will not listen.
But let justice roll down like waters,
and righteousness like an ever-flowing stream.

JUDAISM: Amos 5.23–24

N O ONE can serve two masters; for either he will hate the one and love the other, or he will be devoted to one and despise the other. You cannot serve God and money.

CHRISTIANITY: Matthew 6.24

T HE TRUE believers are those whose hearts are filled with awe at the mention of God, and whose faith grows stronger as they listen to His revelations. They put their trust in their Lord, pray steadfastly, and give in alms of that which We have given them.

Such are the true believers. They shall be exalted and forgiven by their Lord, and a generous provision shall be made for them.

ISLAM: Qur'an 8.2–4

E NTER BY the narrow gate; for the gate is wide and the way is easy that leads to destruction, and those who enter by it are many. For the gate is narrow and the way is hard that leads to life, and those who find it are few.

CHRISTIANITY: *Matthew 7.13–14*

B EWARE THAT this world is not made for you to live forever, you will have to change it for hereafter. God, glory be to Him, has not created you without a purpose and has not left you without duties, obligations, and responsibilities.

ISLAM: *Nahjul Balagha Sermon 67*

A NOVICE ASKED the Buddha, "What is goodness and what is greatness?" The Buddha replied, "To follow the Way and hold to what is true is good. When the will is in conformity with the Way, that is greatness."

BUDDHISM: *Sutra of Forty-two Sections 15*

T WO PATHS lie in front of man. Pondering on them, the wise man chooses the path of joy; the fool takes the path of pleasure.

HINDUISM: Katha Upanishad 2

S AY, IF you love God, follow me, and God will love you, and forgive you all your sins; God is All-forgiving, All-compassionate.

ISLAM: Qur'an 3.31

H OW LOFTY is the station which man, if he but choose to fulfill his high destiny, can attain! To what depths of degradation he can sink, depths which the meanest of creatures have never reached!

BAHÁ'Í FAITH: Gleanings 101

I T MATTERS not whether a man does much or little, if only he directs his heart toward Heaven.

JUDAISM: Talmud

O NE WHO is rich in the enlightenment will not indulge in any sinful action, since his conscience is guided by the intellect fully illumined with Truth.

JAINISM: Acarangasutra

D O NOT try to develop what is natural to man; develop what is natural to Heaven. He who develops Heaven benefits life; he who develops man injures life.

TAOISM: Chuang Tzu 19

T RAIN YOURSELF in godliness; for while bodily training is of some value, godliness is of value in every way, as it holds promise for the present life and also for the life to come.

CHRISTIANITY: 1 Timothy 4.7–8

O MAN! VERILY you are ever toiling on toward your Lord – painfully toiling – but you shall meet Him . . . You shall surely travel from stage to stage.

ISLAM: Qur'an 84.6, 19

THE HUMAN SOUL

B E NOT like those who forgot God, therefore He made them forget their own souls!

T HE BODY is the sheath of the soul.

JUDAISM: *Talmud*

T HE DUST returns to the earth as it was, and the spirit returns to God who gave it.

JUDAISM: *Ecclesiastes 12.7*

T HE KINGDOM of God is not coming with signs to be observed, nor will they say, "Lo, here it is!" or "There!" for behold, the kingdom of God is within you.

CHRISTIANITY: *Luke 17.20–21*

E VERY SOUL that walketh humbly with its God, in this Day, and cleaveth unto Him, shall find itself invested with the honor and glory of all goodly names and stations.

BAHÁ'Í FAITH: *Gleanings 82*

Seeking the Good Pleasure of God

N OT EVERY one who says to Me, "Lord, Lord," shall enter the kingdom of Heaven, but he who does the will of My Father who is in heaven.

CHRISTIANITY: *Matthew 7.21*

G OD HAS promised to believers . . . beautiful mansions in Gardens of everlasting bliss. But the greatest bliss is the good pleasure of God: that is the supreme felicity.

ISLAM: *Qur'an 9.72*

O SON OF the Supreme! To the eternal I call thee, yet thou dost seek that which perisheth. What hath made thee turn away from Our desire and seek thine own?

BAHÁ'Í FAITH: *Arabic Hidden Words 23*

WHOSOEVER KEEPS his duty to God, God will appoint a way out for him, and will provide for him in a way that he cannot foresee. And whosoever puts his trust in God, He will suffice him. Lo! God brings His command to pass. God has set a measure for all things.

ISLAM: *Qur'an 65.2–3*

LET THE words of my mouth, and the meditation of my heart, be acceptable in Thy sight, O Lord, my strength and my redeemer.

JUDAISM: *Psalm 19.14*

THE WAY TO SPIRITUAL GROWTH

*Withdraw into yourself and look. And if you do not find
yourself beautiful as yet, do as the sculptor . . . do not
cease chiselling your sculpture until there shines out on
you the godlike splendor of virtue.*

PLOTINUS: *Man and God*

PRAYER

W HEN WE show favor to a man, he withdraws and turns aside, but when ill touches him then he abounds in prayer.

ISLAM: *Qur'an 41.51*

T HE LORD is near to all who call upon Him,
to all who call upon Him in truth.

JUDAISM: *Psalm 145.18*

WHEN THOU prayest, enter into thy closet, and when thou hast shut the door, pray to thy Father which is in secret.

CHRISTIANITY: *Matthew 6.6*

PRAYER RESTRAINS one from shameful and unjust deeds; and remembrance of God is the greatest thing in life, without doubt.

ISLAM: *Qur'an 29.45*

PRAYER IS the service of the heart.

JUDAISM: *Talmud*

O THOU WHO art turning thy face toward God! Close thine eyes to all things else, and open them to the realm of the All-Glorious. Ask whatsoever thou wishest of Him alone; seek whatsoever thou seekest from Him alone. With a look He granteth a hundred thousand hopes, with a glance He healeth a hundred thousand incurable ills, with a glimpse He layeth balm on every wound, with a nod He freeth the hearts from the shackles of grief . . . Then better for thee to bow down thy head in submission, and put thy trust in the All-Merciful Lord.

BAHÁ'Í FAITH: *Selections from the Writings of 'Abdu'l-Bahá*

MEDITATION

IN THE remembrance of God do hearts find satisfaction.

ISLAM: *Qur'an 13.28*

WORSHIP ME through meditation in the sanctuary of the heart.

HINDUISM: *Srimad Bhagavatam 11.5*

THROUGH THE faculty of meditation man attains to eternal life; through it he receives the breath of the Holy Spirit – the bestowal of the Spirit is given in reflection and meditation. The spirit of man is itself informed and strengthened during meditation; through it affairs of which man knew nothing are unfolded before his view.

BAHÁ'Í FAITH: *Paris Talks*

W HEN MEDITATION is mastered, the mind is unwavering like the flame of a lamp in a windless place. In the still mind, in the depths of meditation, the eternal Self reveals itself. Beholding the Self by means of the Self, an aspirant knows the joy and peace of complete fulfillment. Having attained that abiding joy beyond the senses, revealed in the stilled mind, he never swerves from the central truth. He desires nothing else, and cannot be shaken by the heaviest burden of sorrow. The practice of meditation frees one from all affliction. This is the path of yoga . . .

Wherever the mind wanders, restless and diffuse in its search for satisfaction without, lead it within; train it to rest in the Self. Abiding joy comes to those who still the mind. Freeing themselves from the taint of self-will, with their consciousness unified, they become one with God.

HINDUISM: *Bhagavad Gita 6.18–27*

THERE IS a polish for everything that becomes rusty, and the polish for the heart is the remembrance of God.

ISLAM: *Hadith of Tirmidhi*

THAT HAPPINESS which belongs to a mind which by deep meditation has been washed clear of all impurity and has entered within the Self, cannot be described by words; it can be felt by the inward power only.

HINDUISM: *Maitranyana Brahmana Upanishad*

WITHOUT KNOWLEDGE there is no meditation, without meditation there is no knowledge. He who has knowledge and meditation is near to Nirvana.

BUDDHISM: *Dhammapada 372*

GOOD DEEDS

THOUGH HE recites many a scriptural text, but does not act accordingly, that heedless man is like a cowherd who counts others' cattle. He has no share in the fruits of the religious life.

Though he can recite few scriptural texts, but acts in accordance with the teaching, forsaking lust, hatred, and ignorance, with right awareness and mind well emancipated, not clinging to anything here or in the next life, he shares the fruits of the religious life.

BUDDHISM: *Dhammapada 19–20*

ABU HURAIRA reported God's Messenger as saying, "God does not look at your forms and your possessions, but He looks at your hearts and your deeds."

ISLAM: *Hadith of Muslim*

A MAN WHO does great good, and talks not of it, is on the way to perfection. The man who has accomplished a small good and magnifies it in his speech is worth very little.

BAHÁ'Í FAITH: *Paris Talks*

B E YE doers of the word, and not hearers only. For as the body without the spirit is dead, so faith without works is dead also.

CHRISTIANITY: *James 1.22*

E ASY TO do are things that are bad and not beneficial to oneself, but very very difficult indeed to do is that which is beneficial and good.

BUDDHISM: *Dhammapada 163*

AND WHOSOEVER does deeds of righteousness, be it male or female, believing – they shall enter Paradise, and not be wronged a single date spot.

ISLAM: *Qur'an 4.124*

AS A FLOWER that is lovely and beautiful, but is scentless, even so fruitless is the well-spoken word of one who does not practice it.

BUDDHISM: *Dhammapada 51*

WHATEVER YE do, do all to the glory of God.

CHRISTIANITY: *1 Corinthians 10.31*

WHOEVER, BY a good deed, covers the evil done, such a one illumines this world like the moon freed from clouds.

BUDDHISM: *Dhammapada 173*

SEEK YE for a store of good deeds, men and women! For a store of good deeds is full of salvation.

ZOROASTRIANISM: ZEND AVESTA

THE SIN which makes you sad and repentant is liked better by the Lord than the good deed which turns you vain and conceited.

ISLAM: *Nahjul Balagha, Saying 44*

IN THIS world, aspirants may find enlightenment by two different paths. For the contemplative is the path of knowledge; for the active is the path of self-less action.

HINDUISM: *Bhagavad Gita 3.3*

B E GENEROUS in prosperity, and thankful in adversity. Be worthy of the trust of thy neighbor, and look upon him with a bright and friendly face. Be a treasure to the poor, an admonisher to the rich, an answerer of the cry of the needy, a preserver of the sanctity of thy pledge. Be fair in thy judgment, and guarded in thy speech. Be unjust to no man, and show all meekness to all men. Be as a lamp unto them that walk in darkness, a joy to the sorrowful, a sea for the thirsty, a haven for the distressed, an upholder and defender of the victim of oppression. Let integrity and uprightness distinguish all thine acts. Be a home for the stranger, a balm to the suffering, a tower of strength for the fugitive.

BAHÁ'Í FAITH: *Gleanings 130*

I SAY TO you, Do not resist one who is evil. But if any one strikes you on the right cheek, turn to him the other also; and if any one would sue you and take your coat, let him have your cloak as well; and if any one forces you to go one mile, go with him two miles. Give to him who begs from you, and do not refuse him who would borrow from you.

CHRISTIANITY: *Matthew 5.39–42*

T O REFRAIN from evil, to cultivate good, to purify one's mind – this is the teaching of the Buddhas.

BUDDHISM: *Dhammapada 183*

Self-Cultivation

The Master said, "At fifteen I set my heart upon learning. At thirty, I had planted my feet upon firm ground. At forty, I no longer suffered from perplexities. At fifty, I knew what were the biddings of Heaven. At sixty, I heard them with a docile ear. At seventy, I could follow the dictates of my own heart; for what I desired no longer overstepped the boundaries of right."

CONFUCIANISM: *Analects 2.4*

Birth does not lead to greatness; but the cultivation of virtues by a person leads him to greatness.

JAINISM: *Vajjalagam 687*

ABU HURAIRA reported God's Messenger as saying, "The believers whose faith is most perfect are those who have the best character."

ISLAM: Hadith of Abu Dawud and Darimi

THE LIGHT of a good character surpasseth the light of the sun and the radiance thereof. Whoso attaineth unto it is accounted as a jewel among men.

BAHÁ'Í FAITH: Tablets of Bahá'u'lláh

THE MASTER said, "Even when walking in a party of no more than three I can always be certain of learning from those I am with. There will be good qualities that I can select for imitation and bad ones that will teach me what requires correction in myself."

CONFUCIANISM: ANALECTS 7.21

B Y DEGREES, little by little, from time to time, a wise person should remove his own impurities as a smith removes the dross from silver.

BUDDHISM: Dhammapada 239

M AN MAKES a harness for his beast; all the more should he make one for the beast within himself, his evil desire.

JUDAISM: Talmud

D O NOT say about anything, "I am going to do that tomorrow," without adding, "If God will." Remember your Lord whenever you forget, and say, "Perhaps my Lord will guide me even closer than this to proper conduct."

ISLAM: Qur'an 18.23–24

T HOSE WHO make channels for water control the waters; makers of arrows make the arrows straight; carpenters control their timber; and the holy control their soul.

BUDDHISM: Dhammapada 145

E VERY HUMAN being has been given free-will. If he wishes to incline himself toward the good way and to be righteous, he is free to do so; and if he wishes to incline himself toward the evil way and to be wicked he is free to do that . . . Every individual is capable of being righteous like Moses or wicked like Jeroboam, wise or foolish, merciful or cruel, mean or generous.

JUDAISM: Mishneh Torah 5.1–3

O SON OF Being! Bring thyself to account each day ere thou art summoned to a reckoning; for death, unheralded, shall come upon thee and thou shalt be called to give account for thy deeds.

BAHÁ'Í FAITH: Arabic Hidden Words 31

THE MAN who wisely controls his senses as a good driver controls his horses, and who is free from lower passions and pride, is admired even by the gods; he is calm like the earth that endures; he is steady like a column that is firm; he is pure like a lake that is clear . . . In the light of his vision he has found his freedom: his thoughts are peace, his words are peace, and his work is peace.

BUDDHISM: Dhammapada 94–96

E VEN AS rain breaks through an ill-thatched house, passions will break through an ill-guarded mind . . . Invisible and subtle is the mind, and it flies after fancies wherever it likes; but let the wise man guard well his mind, for a mind well guarded is a source of great joy.

BUDDHISM: *Dhammapada 13, 36*

C ONFUCIUS SAID, "If out of the three hundred Songs I had to take one phrase to cover all my teachings, I would say, 'Let there be no evil in your thoughts.'"

CONFUCIANISM: *Analects 2.2*

WITHOUT GOING out of my door
I can know all things on earth
Without looking out of my window
I can know the ways of heaven.

For the further one travels
The less one knows.

The sage therefore
Arrives without traveling,
Sees all without looking,
Does all without doing.

TAOISM: *Tao Te Ching 47*

INNER PEACE

MAY THE Lord lift up His countenance upon you, and give you peace.

JUDAISM: Numbers 6.26

FOR THE man who forsakes all desires and abandons all pride of possession and of self reaches the goal of peace supreme.

HINDUISM: Bhagavad Gita 2.71

DISCIPLINE, TO be sure, is never pleasant; at times it seems painful, but afterwards those who have been trained by it reap the harvest of a peaceful and upright life.

CHRISTIANITY: Hebrews 12.11

THOU DOST keep him in perfect peace,
whose mind is stayed on Thee,
because he trusts in Thee.

JUDAISM: *Isaiah 26.3*

AND THOSE who in high thought and deep contemplation with ever-living power advance on the path, they in the end reach Nirvana, the peace supreme and infinite joy.

BUDDHISM: *Dhammapada 23*

THE FRUIT of the spirit is love, joy, peace, patience, kindness, generosity, faithfulness, gentleness, and self-control.

CHRISTIANITY: *Galatians 5.22–23*

MEN DO not mirror themselves in running water – they mirror themselves in still water. Only what is still can still the stillness of other things.

TAOISM: *Chuang Tzu 5*

PERSONAL
SPIRITUALITY

A spiritual life is simply a life in which all that we do comes from the centre, where we are anchored in God.

EVELYN UNDERHILL: A Spiritual Life

LOVE

I F I SPEAK in the tongues of men and of angels, but have not love, I am only a resounding gong or a clanging cymbal. If I have the gift of prophecy and can fathom all mysteries and all knowledge, and if I have a faith that can move mountains, but have not love, I am nothing. If I can give all I possess to the poor and surrender my body to the flames, but have not love, I gain nothing.

Love is patient, love is kind. It does not envy, it does not boast, it is not proud. It is not rude, it is not self-seeking, it is not easily angered, it keeps no record of wrongs. Love does not delight in evil but rejoices with the truth. It always protects, always trusts, always hopes, always perseveres.

Love never fails. But where there are prophecies, they will cease; where there are tongues, they will be stilled; where there is knowledge, it will pass away. For we know in part and we prophesy in part, but when perfection comes, the imperfect disappears.

When I was a child, I talked like a child, I thought like a child, I reasoned like a child. When I became a man, I put childish ways behind me. Now we see but a poor reflection as in a mirror; then we shall see face to face. Now I know in part; then I shall know fully, even as I am fully known.

And now these three remain: faith, hope, and love. But the greatest of these is love.

CHRISTIANITY: *1 Corinthians 13.1–13*

TREAT PEOPLE in such a way and live amongst them in such a manner that if you die they will weep over you; alive they crave for your company.

ISLAM: *Nahjul Balagha, Saying 9*

YOU HAVE heard that it was said, "You shall love your neighbor and hate your enemy." But I say to you, Love your enemies and pray for those who persecute you, so that you may be sons of your Father who is in heaven; for He makes His sun rise on the evil and on the good, and sends rain on the just and on the unjust.

CHRISTIANITY: *Matthew 5.43–45*

I F MEN speak evil of you, this must you think: "Our heart shall not waver; and we will abide in compassion, in loving-kindness, without resentment. We will think of the man who speaks ill of us with thoughts of love, and in our thoughts of love shall we dwell. And from that abode of love we will fill the whole world with far-reaching, wide-spreading, boundless love."

Moreover, if robbers should attack you and cut you in pieces with a two-handed saw, limb by limb, and one of you should feel hate, such a one is not a follower of my gospel.

BUDDHISM: *Majjhima Nikaya*

O NLY BY love can men see me, and know me, and come unto me.

HINDUISM: *Bhagavad Gita 11.54*

A DISCIPLE HAVING asked for a definition of charity, the Master said "Love one another."

CONFUCIANISM: *Analects*

K NOW THOU of a certainty that love is the secret of God's holy dispensation, the manifestation of the All-Merciful, the fountain of spiritual outpourings. Love is heaven's kindly light, the Holy Spirit's eternal breath that vivifieth the human soul. Love is the cause of God's revelation unto man, the vital bond inherent, in accordance with the divine creation, in the realities of things. Love is the one means that ensureth true felicity both in this world and the next. Love is the light that guideth in darkness, the living link that uniteth God with man, that assureth the progress of every illumined soul.

BAHÁ'Í FAITH: *Selections from the writings of 'Abdu'l-Bahá*

FAITH

H E THAT hath faith hath wisdom; he that hath wisdom hath peace. He that hath no wisdom and no faith, whose soul is one of doubt, is destroyed.

BUDDHISM: *Mahabharata*

F OR TRULY, I say to you, if you have faith as a grain of mustard seed, you will say to this mountain, "Move from here to there," and it will move; and nothing will be impossible to you.

CHRISTIANITY: *Matthew 17.20*

GENEROSITY

THERE ARE three kinds of persons existing in the world: one is like a drought, one who rains locally, and one who pours down everywhere.

How is a person like a drought? He gives nothing to all alike, not giving food and drink, clothing and vehicle, flowers, scents, and unguents, bed, lodging, and light, neither to recluses and brahmins nor to wretched and needy beggars. In this way, a person is like a drought.

How is a person like a local rainfall? He is a giver to some, but to others he gives not . . . In this way, a person is like a local rainfall.

How does a person rain down everywhere? He gives to all, be they recluses and brahmins or wretched, needy beggars; he is a giver of food and drink, clothing . . . lodging and lights. In this way a person rains down everywhere.

BUDDHISM: *Itivuttaka 65*

GIVE, AND it will be given to you . . . For the measure you give will be the measure you get back.

CHRISTIANITY: *Luke 6.38*

A MAN OF humanity is one who, in seeking to establish himself, finds a foothold for others and who, desiring attainment for himself, helps others to attain.

CONFUCIANISM: *Analects*

THE GIFT which is given without thought of recompense, in the belief that it ought to be made, in a fit place, at an opportune time, and to a deserving person – such a gift is Pure.

That which is given for the sake of the results it will produce, or with the hope of recompense, or grudgingly – that may truly be said to be an outcome of Passion.

HINDUISM: *Bhagavad Gita 17.20–21*

BE GENEROUS but not extravagant, be frugal but not miserly.

ISLAM: *Nahjul Balagha, Saying 32*

I F BEINGS knew, as I know, the fruit of sharing gifts, they would not enjoy their use without sharing them, nor would the taint of stinginess obsess the heart and stay there. Even if it were their last bit, their last morsel of food, they would not enjoy its use without sharing it, if there were anyone to receive it.

BUDDHISM: *Itivuttaka 18*

T HOSE WHO contribute their wealth in the way of God are like a grain which produces seven ears in each of which are a hundred grains. God gives double to whom He wills.

ISLAM: *Qur'an 2.263*

C HARITY KNOWS no race, no creed.

JUDAISM: *Talmud*

G IVE TO him who begs from you, and do not refuse him who would borrow from you.

CHRISTIANITY: *Matthew 5.42*

PURITY

C ONFUCIUS SAID, "A faultless man I cannot hope ever to meet; the most I can hope for is to meet a man of fixed principles."

CONFUCIANISM: *Analects 7.25*

B EWARE OF practicing your piety before men in order to be seen by them; for then you have no reward from your Father who is in heaven.

CHRISTIANITY: *Matthew 6.1*

P URITY AND stillness are the correct principles for mankind.

TAOISM: *Sayings of Lao-tzu*

B Y ONE'S Self one becomes pure. The pure and impure stand and fall by their own deeds; no one can purify another.

BUDDHISM: *Dhammapada 165*

SAMSARA, THE transmigration of life,
takes place in one's mind.
Let one therefore keep the mind pure,
for what one thinks, that he becomes:
this is the mystery of Eternity.

HINDUISM: *Maitri Upanishad*

W HAT WE are today comes from our thoughts of yesterday, and our present thoughts build our life of tomorrow: our life is the creation of our mind.

If a man speaks or acts with an impure mind, suffering follows him as the wheel of a cart follows the beast that draws the cart . . .

If a man speaks or acts with a pure mind, joy follows him as his own shadow.

BUDDHISM: *Dhammapada 1–2*

A s A MAN thinketh in his heart, so is he.

JUDAISM: *Proverbs 23.7*

FORGIVENESS

T HE BEST deed of a great man is to forgive and forget.

ISLAM: *Nahjul Balagha, Saying 201*

B E TOLERANT of one another and forgiving; if any of you has cause for complaint, you must forgive as the Lord forgave you.

CHRISTIANITY: *Colossians 3.13*

T HE SUPERIOR man tends to forgive wrongs and deals leniently with crimes.

CONFUCIANISM: *I Ching 40*

J UDGE NOT, and you will not be judged; condemn not, and you will not be condemned; forgive, and you will be forgiven.

CHRISTIANITY: *Luke 6.3*

M OSES SON of 'Imran said, "My Lord, who is the greatest of Thy servants in Thy estimation?" and received the reply, "The one who forgives when he is in a position of power."

ISLAM: *Hadith of Baihaqi*

HONESTY

THERE IS no evil that cannot be done by a lying person who has trangressed the one law [of truthfulness] and who is indifferent to a world beyond.

BUDDHISM: *Dhammapada 176*

THEN HAVE done with falsehood and speak the truth to each other, for we belong to one another as parts of one body.

CHRISTIANITY: *Ephesians 4.25*

TRUTHFULNESS IS the foundation of all human virtues. Without truthfulness, progress and success, in all the worlds of God, are impossible for any soul. When this holy attribute is established in man, all the divine qualities will also be acquired.

BAHÁ'Í FAITH: *Advent of Divine Justice*

MASTER TSENG said, "Every day I examine myself . . . In intercourse with my friends, have I always been true to my word?"

CONFUCIANISM: *Analects 1.4*

HUMILITY

ALL AROUND I see Nothing pretending to be Something, Emptiness pretending to be Fulness.

CONFUCIANISM: *Analects 7.25*

PRIDE GOES before destruction,
and a haughty spirit before a fall.

JUDAISM: *Proverbs 16.18*

HUMILITY EXALTETH man to the heaven of glory and power, whilst pride abaseth him to the depths of wretchedness and degradation.

BAHÁ'Í FAITH: *Epistle to the Son of the Wolf*

DO NOT walk boisterously upon the earth; verily thou wilt not make a hole in the earth, nor yet reach the mountains in stature.

ISLAM: *Qur'an 17.39*

CONTENTMENT

A SERENE SPIRIT accepts pleasure and pain with an even mind, and is unmoved by either. He alone is worthy of immortality.

HINDUISM: *Bhagavad Gita 2.15*

THERE IS no crime greater than having too many desires;
There is no disaster greater than not being content;
There is no misfortune greater than being covetous.

TAOISM: *Tao Te Ching 46*

THOUGH THE fig tree does not blossom,
nor fruit be on the vines,
the produce of the olive fail,
and the fields yield no food,
the flock be cut off from the fold,
and there be no herd in the stalls,
yet I will rejoice in the Lord,
I will exult in the God of my salvation.

JUDAISM: *Habakkuk 3.17–18*

Selflessness

D o nothing from selfishness or conceit, but in humility count others better than yourselves. Let each of you look not only to his own interests, but also to the interests of others.

Christianity: Philippians 2.3–4

W oe to those who are wise in their own eyes, and shrewd in their own sight!

Judaism: Isaiah 5.21

C onfucius said, "The good man does not grieve that other people do not recognize his merits. His only anxiety is lest he should fail to recognize theirs."

Confucianism: Analects 1.16

A S A SOLID rock is not shaken by the wind, even so the wise are not ruffled by praise or blame.

BUDDHISM: *Dhammapada 6*

WHOEVER PROCLAIMS himself good,
know, goodness approaches him not.

SIKHISM: *Adi Granth, Gauri Sukhmani M.5*

O MY SERVANT! Free thyself from the fetters of this world, and loose thy soul from the prison of self. Seize thy chance, for it will come to thee no more.

BAHÁ'Í FAITH: *Persian Hidden Words 40*

COMPASSION

O ACT like the beasts of the field is unworthy of man. Those virtues that befit his dignity are forbearance, mercy, compassion, and loving-kindness toward all the peoples and kindreds of the earth.

BAHÁ'Í FAITH: *Gleanings 109*

HO IS incapable of hatred toward any being, who is kind and compassionate, free from selfishness . . . such a devotee of Mine is My beloved.

HINDUISM: *Bhagavad Gita 12.13–14*

E OF one mind, sympathetic, loving toward one another, compassionate, humble. Do not return evil for evil, or insult for insult; but on the contrary, a blessing, because to this you were called, that you might inherit a blessing.

CHRISTIANITY: *1 Peter 3.8–9*

PATIENCE

P ATIENCE, FORBEARANCE, always wins out, not anger. One who is patient becomes established in the absolute.

BUDDHISM: *Mahabharata*

B E HUMBLE always and gentle, and patient too, putting up with one another's failings in a spirit of love.

CHRISTIANITY: *Ephesians 4.2*

B E PATIENT under all conditions, and place your whole trust and confidence in God.

BAHÁ'Í FAITH: *Gleanings 136*

O YOU WHO believe, seek courage in fortitude and prayer, for God is with those who are patient and persevere.

ISLAM: QUR'AN 2.153

DETACHMENT

B E IN THE world as if you were a stranger or a traveler.
ISLAM: *Forty Hadith of an–Nawawi 40*

T HE MAN who, casting off all desires, lives free from attachment; who is free from egoism and from the feeling that this or that is mine, obtains tranquillity.
HINDUISM: *Bhagavad Gita 2.71*

F ROM CRAVING springs sorrow and from craving springs fear. If a man is to free himself from craving, he is free from fear and sorrow.
BUDDHISM: *Dhammapada 216*

T HE WORLD is but a show, vain and empty, a mere nothing, bearing the semblance of reality. Set not your affections upon it.
BAHÁ'Í FAITH: *Gleanings 153*

EMPTY THE BOAT of your life, O man; when empty it will swiftly sail. When empty of passions and harmful desires you are bound for the land of Nirvana.

BUDDHISM: *Dhammapada 369*

DO NOT RACE after riches, do not risk your life for success, or you will let slip the Heaven within you.

TAOISM: *Chuang Tzu 29*

HE WHO LOVES his life loses it, and he who hates his life in this world will keep it for eternal life.

CHRISTIANITY: *John 12.25*

JUSTICE

O SON OF SPIRIT! The best beloved of all things in My sight is Justice; turn not away therefrom if thou desirest Me, and neglect it not that I may confide in thee. By its aid thou shalt see with thine own eyes and not through the eyes of others, and shalt know of thine own knowledge and not through the knowledge of thy neighbor.

BAHÁ'Í FAITH: *Arabic Hidden Words 2*

S TAND FAST to Justice, when you bear witness, though it is against yourself, or your parents, or your kin, rich or poor. God is nearer to you than any.
    Therefore follow not passion, lest you swerve from the Truth.

ISLAM: *Qur'an 4.135*

KINDNESS

D O NOT NEGLECT to show hospitality to strangers, for thereby some have entertained angels unawares.

CHRISTIANITY: *Hebrews 13.2*

T HOSE WHO act kindly in this world will have kindness.

ISLAM: *Qur'an 39.10*

D O NOT BE content with showing friendship in words alone, let your heart burn with loving-kindness for all who may cross your path.

BAHÁ'Í FAITH: *Paris Talks*

L ET NO ONE seek his own good, but the good of his neighbor.

CHRISTIANITY: *1 Corinthians 10.24*

L OVING-KINDNESS is greater than laws; and the charities of life are more than all ceremonies.

JUDAISM: *Talmud*

A MAN IS NOT a great man because he is a warrior and kills other men, but because he hurts not any living being he in truth is called a great man.

BUDDHISM: *Dhammapada 270*

SERVICE

THE BEST of men are those who are useful to others.

ISLAM: *Hadith of Bukhari*

BEAR ONE another's burdens, and so fulfill the law of Christ.

CHRISTIANITY: *Galatians 6.2*

MAN'S MERIT lieth in service and virtue and not in the pageantry of wealth and riches.

BAHÁ'Í FAITH: *Tablets of Bahá'u'lláh*

MATERIALISM

THE LOVE OF money is the root of all evils.

CHRISTIANITY: I Timothy 6.10

HE WHO LOVES money will not be satisfied with money; nor he who loves wealth, with gain: this also is vanity.

JUDAISM: Ecclesiastes 5.10

HE WHO considers wealth a good thing can never bear to give up his income; he who considers eminence a good thing can never bear to give up his fame. He who has a taste for power can never bear to hand over authority to others. Holding tight to these things, such men shiver with fear; should they let them go, they would pine in sorrow. They never stop for a moment of reflection, never cease to gaze with greedy eyes – they are men punished by Heaven.

TAOISM: Chuang Tzu 14

T HE WISE do not call strong the fetter that is made of iron, wood, or rope; much stronger is the fetter of passion for gold and jewels, for sons or for wives . . Wealth destroys the fool who seeks not the Beyond.

BUDDHISM: *Dhammapada 345, 355*

E VEN WERE the wealth of the entire world bestowed lavishly on a man, he would not be happy: contentment is difficult to attain.

JAINISM: *Uttaradhyayana Sutra 8 16*

JUDGING OTHERS

EASILY SEEN are others' faults, hard indeed to see are one's own. Like chaff one winnows others' faults, but one's own one hides, as a crafty fowler conceals himself by camouflage.

BUDDHISM: *Dhammapada 252*

FIGHT THINE own sins, not the sins of others.

CONFUCIANISM: *Analects*

JUDGE NOT, that you be not judged. For with the judgment that you pronounce you will be judged, and the measure you give will be the measure you get. Why do you see the speck that is in your brother's eye, but do not notice the log that is in your own eye? . . . First take the log out of your own eye, and then you will see clearly to take the speck out of your brother's eye.

CHRISTIANITY: *Matthew 7.1–5*

T HINK NOT of the faults of others, of what they have done or not done. Think rather of your own sins, of the things you have done or not done.

BUDDHISM: *Dhammapada 50*

O SON OF BEING! How couldst thou forget thine own faults and busy thyself with the faults of others? Whoso doeth this is accursed of Me.

BAHÁ'Í FAITH: *Arabic Hidden Words 26*

BACKBITING

F IND NOT fault with one another, neither revile one another by nicknames . . . O ye believers, eschew much suspicion, for some suspicion is a sin. And do not spy, neither backbite one another.

ISLAM: *Qur'an 49.11–12*

B ROOD OF VIPERS! How can you, being evil, speak good things? For out of the abundance of the heart the mouth speaks. A good man out of the good treasure of his heart brings forth good things, and an evil man out of the evil treasure brings forth evil things. But I say to you that for every idle word men may speak, they will give account of it in the day of judgment. For by your words you will be justified, and by your words you will be condemned.

CHRISTIANITY: *Matthew 12.34–37*

LORD, WHO shall abide in Thy Tabernacle?
Who shall dwell in Thy holy hill?
He that backbiteth not with his tongue
nor doeth evil to his neighbor.

JUDAISM: *Psalm 15.1,3*

B ACKBITING QUENCHETH the light of the heart, and
extinguisheth the life of the soul.

BAHÁ'Í FAITH: *Gleanings 125*

G OOD IS restraint in speech . . . [he] who is controlled
in tongue, who speaks wisely . . . sweet, indeed, is
his speech.

BUDDHISM: *Dhammapada 363*

Personal Spirituality ❧ *101*

THE GOLDEN RULE

YOU SHALL love your neighbor as yourself.

JUDAISM: *Leviticus 19.18*

TSEKUNG ASKED, "Is there one word that can serve as a principle of conduct for life?" Confucius replied, "It is the word shu – reciprocity: Do not do to others what you do not want them to do to you."

CONFUCIANISM: *Analects 15.23*

HURT NOT others with that which pains yourself.

BUDDHISM: *Udana 5.18*

NOT ONE of you is a believer until he loves for his brother what he loves for himself.

ISLAM: Forty Hadith of an-Nawawi 13

DESIRE NOT for anyone the things that ye would not desire for yourselves.

BAHÁ'Í FAITH: Gleanings 66

ALL THINGS whatsoever ye would that men should do to you, do ye even so to them: for this is the law and the prophets.

CHRISTIANITY:: Matthew 7.12

NEVER DO to others what would pain thyself.

HINDUISM: *Panchatantra 3.104*

TREAT OTHERS as thou wouldst be treated thyself.

SIKHISM: *Adi Granth*

REGARD YOUR neighbor's gain as your own gain and your neighbor's loss as your own loss.

TAOISM: *T'ai Shang Kan Ying P'ien*

THAT NATURE only is good when it shall not do unto another whatever is not good for its own self.

ZOROASTRIANISM: *Dadistan-i-Dinik*

FAMILY AND COMMUNITY LIFE

Life is short. Be swift to love!
Make haste to be kind!

HENRI F. AMIEL

Marriage

NOT THOSE are true husband and wife that with each other [merely] consort: Truly wedded are those that in two frames, are as one light.

SIKHISM: *Adi Granth, Var Suhi M.3*

I AM HE, you are She;
I am Song, you are Verse,
I am Heaven, you are Earth.
We two shall here together dwell,
becoming parents of children.

HINDUISM: ATHARVA VEDA 14.2.71

THE MORAL man finds the moral law beginning in the relation between man and woman, but ending in the vast reaches of the universe.

CONFUCIANISM: *Doctrine of the Mean 12*

AMONG HIS signs is that He created spouses for you among yourselves that you may console yourselves with them. He has planted affection and mercy between you.

ISLAM: *Qur'an 30.21*

HE WHO loves his wife as himself; who honors her more than himself; who rears his children in the right path, and who marries them off at the proper time of their life, concerning him it is written:"And you will know that your home is at peace."

JUDAISM: *Talmud*

BE SUBJECT to one another out of reverence for Christ.

CHRISTIANITY: *Ephesians 5.21*

T HE LORD, peerless is He, hath made woman and man to abide with each other in the closest companionship, and to be even as a single soul. They are two helpmates, two intimate friends, who should be concerned about the welfare of each other.

If they live thus, they will pass through this world with perfect contentment, bliss, and peace of heart, and become the object of divine grace and favor in the Kingdom of heaven . . . Strive, then, to abide, heart and soul, with each other as two doves in the nest, for this is to be blessed in both worlds.

BAHÁ'Í FAITH: *Selections from the Writings of 'Abdu'l-Bahá*

A GOOD wife who can find?
She is far more precious than jewels.
The heart of her husband trusts in her,
   and he will have no lack of gain.
She does him good, and not harm,
   all the days of her life.

JUDAISM: *Proverbs 31.10–11*

CHILDREN

TRAIN UP a child in the way he should go,
and when he is old he will not depart from it.

JUDAISM: PROVERBS 22.6

F rom the very beginning, the children must receive divine education and must continually be reminded to remember their God. Let the love of God pervade their inmost being, commingled with their mother's milk.

BAHÁ'Í FAITH: *Selections from the Writings of 'Abdu'l-Bahá*

HE WHO spares the rod hates his son,
but he who loves him is diligent to discipline him.

JUDAISM: *Proverbs 13.24*

A s THE CHILD, according to its natural disposition, commits thousands of faults, The father instructs and slights, but again hugs him to his bosom.

SIKHISM: *Adi Granth, Sorath M.5*

PARENTS

T HY LORD has decreed . . . that you be kind to parents. Whether one or both of them attain old age in your lifetime, do not say to them a word of contempt, nor repel them, but address them in terms of honor. And, out of kindness, lower to them the wing of humility, and say, "My Lord! bestow on them Thy mercy even as they cherished me in childhood."

ISLAM: *Qur'an 17.23*

S UPPORTING ONE'S father and mother, cherishing wife and children and a peaceful occupation; that is the greatest blessing.

BUDDHISM: *Sutta Nipata 262*

T HERE ARE three partners in man, God, father, and mother. When a man honors his father and mother, God says, "I regard it as though I had dwelt among them and they had honored me."

JUDAISM: *Talmud*

O NE COMPANION asked, "O Apostle of God! Who is the person worthiest of my consideration?" He replied, "Your mother." He asked again, "And second to my mother?" The Prophet said, "Your mother." The companion insisted, "And then?" The Messenger of God said, "After your mother, your father."

ISLAM: *Hadith of Bukhari and Muslim*

I T IS SEEMLY that the servant should, after each prayer, supplicate God to bestow mercy and forgiveness upon his parents. Thereupon God's call will be raised: "Thousand upon thousand of what thou hast asked for thy parents shall be thy recompense!" Blessed is he who remembereth his parents when communing with God. There is, verily, no God but Him, the Mighty, the Well-Beloved.

BAHÁ'Í FAITH: *Selections from the Writings of the Báb*

H ONOR YOUR father and your mother that your days may be long in the land which the Lord your God gives you.

JUDAISM: *Exodus 20.12*

FRIENDS

G REATER LOVE has no man than this, that a man lay down his life for his friends.

CHRISTIANITY: John 15.13

C ONFUCIUS SAID, "There are three sorts of friend that are profitable, and three sorts that are harmful. Friendship with the upright, with the true-to-death, and with those who have heard much is profitable. Friendship with the obsequious, friendship with those who are good at accommodating their principles, friendship with those who are clever at talk is harmful."

CONFUCIANISM: Analects 16.4

WHEN TWO people are at one in their inmost hearts,
They shatter even the strength of iron or of bronze.
And when two people understand each other in their
  inmost hearts,
Their words are sweet and strong, like the fragrance of orchids.

CONFUCIANISM: *I Ching*

I F YOU DESIRE with all your heart, friendship with
every race on earth, your thought, spiritual and
positive, will spread; it will become the desire of
others, growing stronger and stronger, until it
reaches the minds of all men.

BAHÁ'Í FAITH: *Paris Talks*

T HERE ARE friends who pretend to be friends, but
there is a friend who sticks closer than a brother.

JUDAISM: *Proverbs 18.24*

I T IS ONLY when one does not have enough faith in
others that others will have no faith in him.

TAOISM: *Tao Te Ching 17*

S EEK FOR friends those who are good; that will help you to practice virtue with body and soul. Keep at a distance those who are wicked; it will prevent evil from approaching you.

TAOISM: *Tract of the Quiet Way*

H E WHO entreats aid for his comrade, though he himself is in need, is answered first.

JUDAISM: *Talmud*

H AVE NOT for friends those whose soul is ugly; go not with men who have an evil soul. Have for friends those whose soul is beautiful; go with those whose soul is good.

BUDDHISM: *Dhammapada 78*

CARING FOR THE NEEDY

WHOEVER REMOVES a worldly grief from a believer, Allah will remove from him one of the griefs on the day of judgment. Whosoever alleviates the lot of a needy person, Allah will alleviate his lot in this world and the next. Whosoever shields a Muslim, Allah will shield him in this world and the next. Allah will aid a servant of His so long as the servant aids his brother.

ISLAM: *Forty Hadith of an-Nawawi 36*

RELIEVE PEOPLE in distress as speedily as you must release a fish from a dry rill. Deliver people from danger as quickly as you must free a sparrow from a tight noose. Be compassionate to orphans and relieve widows. Respect the old and help the poor.

TAOISM: *Tract of the Quiet Way*

BLESSED IS he who considers the poor;
the Lord delivers him in the day of trouble.

JUDAISM: *Psalm 41.1*

LET THE RICH man satisfy one who seeks help;
and let him look upon the long view:
For wealth revolves like the wheels of a chariot,
coming now to one, now to another.

HINDUISM: *Rig Veda 10.117.5*

O N THE DAY of judgment God Most High will say, "Son of Adam, I was sick and you did not visit Me." He will reply, "My Lord, how could I visit Thee when Thou art the Lord of the Universe!" He will say, "Did you not know that My servant so-and-so was ill and yet you did not visit him? Did you not know that if you had visited him you soon would have found Me with him?"

ISLAM: *Hadith of Muslim*

O YE RICH Ones on Earth! The poor in your midst are My trust; guard ye My trust, and be not intent only on your own ease . . . To give and to be generous are attributes of Mine; well is it with him that adorneth himself with My virtues.

Baháʼí Faith: Persian Hidden Words 54

H E WHO HAS two coats, let him share with him who has none; and he who has food, let him do likewise.

Christianity: Luke 3.11

W HEN THE Holy One loves a man, He sends him a present in the shape of a poor man, so that he should perform some good deed to him, through the merit of which he may draw to himself a cord of grace.

Judaism: Zohar, Genesis 104a

Respecting Elders

F OR ONE who frequently honors and respects elders, four things increase: age, beauty, bliss, and strength.

BUDDHISM: *Dhammapada 109*

Y OU SHALL rise up before the hoary head, and honor the face of an old man, and you shall fear God: I am the Lord.

JUDAISM: *Leviticus 19.32*

EQUALITY

NDER THE Guru's instruction regard all men as equal, since God's light is contained in the heart of each.

SIKHISM: *Arjan*

CHILDREN OF Men! Know ye not why We created you all from the same dust? That no one should exalt himself over the other.

BAHÁ'Í FAITH: *Arabic Hidden Words 68*

E MAKES his sun rise on the evil and on the good, and sends rain on the just and on the unjust.

CHRISTIANITY: *Matthew 5.45*

H AVE WE not all one father? Has not one God created us all? Why then do we deal treacherously, every man against his brother, and profane the Covenant of our fathers?

JUDAISM: *Malachi 2.10*

R ELIGION CONSISTETH not in mere words; he who looketh on all men as equal is religious.

SIKHISM: *Guru Nanak*

THERE IS neither Jew nor Greek, there is neither slave nor free, there is neither male nor female; for you are all one in Christ Jesus.

CHRISTIANITY: *Galatians 3.28*

UNITY

I T IS NOT for him to pride himself who loveth his own country, but rather for him who loveth the whole world. The earth is but one country, and mankind its citizens.

BAHÁ'Í FAITH: *Gleanings 117*

O MANKIND! We created you from a single pair of a male and a female and made you into nations and tribes, that you might know each other. Verily the most honored among you in the sight of God is he who is the most righteous.

ISLAM: *Qur'an 49.13*

HE WHO experiences the unity of life, sees his own self in all beings, and all beings in his own self, and looks on everything with an impartial eye.

HINDUISM: *Bhagavad Gita 6.29*

HOLD FAST, all together, to God's rope, and be not divided amongst yourselves . . . Let there arise out of you one community, inviting to all that is good, enjoining what is right, and forbidding what is wrong: those will be prosperous.

ISLAM: *Qur'an 3:103–5*

EVERY KINGDOM divided against itself is laid waste, and no city or house divided against itself will stand.

CHRISTIANITY: *Matthew 12.25*

YE ARE all the fruits of one tree and the leaves of one branch. Deal ye one with another with the utmost love and harmony, with friendliness and fellowship . . . So powerful is the light of unity that it can illuminate the whole earth.

BAHÁ'Í FAITH: *Gleanings 132*

CONSIDER THE family of humankind one.

JAINISM: *Jinasena, Adipurana*

MEET TOGETHER, speak together,
let your minds be of one accord,
as the Gods of old, being of one mind,
accepted their share of the sacrifice.

May your counsel be common, your assembly common,
common the mind, and the thoughts of these united.
A common purpose do I lay before you,
and worship with your common oblation.

Let your aims be common,
and your hearts of one accord,
and all of you be of one mind,
so you may live well together.

HINDUISM: *Rig Veda 10.191.2–4*

I CHARGE you all that each one of you concentrate all the thoughts of your heart on love and unity. When a thought of war comes, oppose it by a stronger thought of peace. A thought of hatred must be destroyed by a more powerful thought of love. Thoughts of war bring destruction to all harmony, well-being, restfulness and content . . . Thoughts of love are constructive of brotherhood, peace, friendship, and happiness.

BAHÁ'Í FAITH: *Paris Talks*

W HOEVER CAN protest against the injustices of his family but refrains from doing so, should be punished for the crimes of his family. Whoever can protest against the injustices of the people of his community, but refrains from doing so, should be punished for the crimes of his community. Whoever is able to protest against the injustices of the entire world but refrains from doing so, should be punished for the crimes of the whole world.

JUDAISM: *Talmud*

TROUBLES, TESTS, AND DIFFICULTIES

*The gem cannot be polished without friction, nor man
perfected without trials.*

CHINESE PROVERB

Suffering and Grief

BLESSED ARE those who mourn, for they shall be comforted.

CHRISTIANITY: *Matthew 5.4*

A CHEERFUL heart is a good medicine.

JUDAISM: *Proverbs 17.22*

SURELY GOD wrongs not men anything, but men wrong themselves.

ISLAM: *Qur'an 10.44*

T HIS BODY is mortal, always gripped by death, but within it dwells the immortal Self. This Self, when associated in our consciousness with the body, is subject to pleasure and pain; and so long as this association continues, freedom from pleasure and pain can no man find.

HINDUISM: *Chandogya Unpanishad 8.12.1*

O MY SERVANTS! Sorrow not if, in these days and on this earthly plane, things contrary to your wishes have been ordained and manifested by God, for days of blissful joy, of heavenly delight, are assuredly in store for you.

BAHÁ'Í FAITH: *Gleanings 153*

THE LORD is my shepherd; I shall not want.
He maketh me to lie down in green pastures:
He leadeth me beside the still waters.
He restoreth my soul: He leadeth me in the paths
of righteousness for His name's sake.
Yea, though I walk through the valley of the
shadow of death, I will fear no evil:
for Thou art with me; Thy rod and Thy
staff they comfort me.
Thou preparest a table before me in the presence
of mine enemies: Thou anointest my head
with oil; my cup runneth over.
Surely goodness and mercy shall follow me all
the days of my life: and I will dwell in the
house of the Lord for ever.

JUDAISM: *Psalm 23*

B Y ONESELF alone is evil done; it is self-born, it is self-caused. Evil grinds the unwise as a diamond grinds a hard gem.

BUDDHISM: Dhammapada 161

C OME TO ME, all who labor and are heavy laden, and I will give you rest.

CHRISTIANITY: Matthew 11.28

HE HEALS the brokenhearted,
and binds up their wounds.

JUDAISM: Psalm 147.3

TESTS

D O MEN imagine that they will be left because they say, "We believe," and will not be tested with affliction? Lo! We tested those who were before you. Thus God knows those who are sincere, and knows those who feign.

ISLAM: *Qur'an 29.2–3*

T ESTS ARE benefits from God, for which we should thank Him. Grief and sorrow do not come to us by chance; they are sent to us by the divine mercy for our own perfecting . . .

Men who suffer not, attain no perfection. The plant most pruned by the gardeners is that one which, when the summer comes, will have the most beautiful blossoms and the most abundant fruit.

The laborer cuts up the earth with his plough, and from that earth comes the rich and plentiful harvest. The more a man is chastened, the greater is the harvest of spiritual virtues shown forth by him. A soldier is no good general until he has been in the front of the fiercest battle and has received the deepest wounds.

BAHÁ'Í FAITH: *Paris Talks*

Overcoming Anger, Hatred, and Envy

C ONQUER ANGER by love. Conquer evil by good. Conquer the mean by generosity. Conquer the liar by truth . . . Never in the world is hatred conquered by hatred: hatred is conquered by love.

HINDUISM: *Dhammapada 223, 5*

BE SWIFT to hear, slow to speak, slow to wrath.

CHRISTIANITY: *James 1.19*

W HOEVER SEES all beings in himself and himself in all beings does not, by virtue of such realization, hate anyone . . . When, to that wise sage, all beings are realized as existing in his own self, then what illusion, what sorrow, can afflict him, perceiving as he does the Unity?

HINDUISM: *Isa Upanishads*

HE WHO IS slow to anger is better than the mighty,

And he who who rules his spirit than he who takes a city.

JUDAISM: *Proverbs 16.32*

EACH OF YOU should examine your own conduct, and then he can measure his achievement by comparing himself to himself and not with anyone else; for everyone has his own burden to bear.

CHRISTIANITY: Galatians 6.4

MAN SHOULD subvert anger by forgiveness, subdue pride by modesty, overcome hypocrisy with simplicity, and greed by contentment.

JAINISM: Samanasuttam 136

A SOFT answer turns away wrath,
but a harsh word stirs up anger.

JUDAISM: Proverbs 15.1

DO NOT SPEAK harshly to anybody; those who are spoken to will answer thee in the same way. Angry speech breeds trouble; thou wilt receive blows for blows.

BUDDHISM: Dhammapada 133

OVERCOMING ANXIETY AND FEAR

D O NOT be anxious about anything, but in everything, by prayer and petition, with thanksgiving, present your requests to God. And the peace of God, which transcends all understanding, will guard your hearts and your minds in Christ Jesus.

CHRISTIANITY: *Philippians 4.6–7*

HEAR MY cry, O God;
    listen to my prayer.
From the ends of the earth I call to you,
    I call as my heart grows faint;
    lead me to the rock that is higher than I.
For you have been my refuge,
    a strong tower against the foe
I long to dwell in your tent for ever
    and take refuge in the shelter of your wings.

JUDAISM: *Psalm 61.1–4*

LIFE AFTER DEATH

That day which you fear as being the end of all things is the birthday of your eternity.

SENECA

DEATH

N OT IN THE sky, nor deep in the ocean, nor in a mountain cave is there a spot in the whole world where, if a man abide there, death could not overtake him.

BUDDHISM: *Dhammapada 128*

As a man passes from dream to wakefulness, so does he pass from this life to the next.

HINDUISM: *Brihadaranyaka Upanishad 4.3.35*

Look upon life as a swelling tumor, a protruding goiter, and upon death as the draining of a sore or the bursting of a boil.

TAOISM *Chuang Tzu 6*

OSon of the Supreme! I have made death a messenger of joy to thee. Wherefore dost thou grieve?

BAHÁ'Í FAITH: *Arabic Hidden Words 32*

A T THE MOMENT of death the sum of all the experiences of life on earth comes to the surface of the mind – for in the mind are stored all impressions of past deeds – and the dying man then becomes absorbed in these experiences. Then comes complete loss of memory. Next there arises before man's mind the vision of his life to come, a vision regulated by his impressions of his past deeds; and he no longer recollects his life on earth. This complete forgetfulness of his past identity is death.

HINDUISM: *Srimad Bhagavatam 11.15*

T RULY, TRULY I say to you, unless a grain of wheat falls into the earth and dies, it remains alone; but if it dies, it bears much fruit.

CHRISTIANITY: *John 12.24*

F OR CERTAIN is death for the born, and certain is birth for the dead; therefore over the inevitable thou shouldst not grieve.

HINDUISM: *Bhagavad Gita 2.27*

O NE WHO identifies himself with his soul regards the transmigration of his soul at death fearlessly, like changing one cloth for another.

JAINISM: *Pujyapada, Samadhishataka 77*

IMMORTALITY

A LL THE LIVING must die, and dying, return to the ground; this is what is called *kuei*. The bones and flesh molder below, and, hidden away, become the earth of the fields. But the spirit issues forth, and is displayed on high in a condition of glorious brightness.

CONFUCIANISM: *Book of Ritual 21.2.1*

THE BODY dies but the spirit is not entombed.

BUDDHISM: *Dhammapada 151*

I T IS NOT born, nor does it ever die, nor having come to be will it ever more come not to be. Unborn, eternal, everlasting, this ancient one [soul] is not slain when the body is slain.

HINDUISM: *Bhagavad Gita 2.20*

W OE IS HE . . . who has gathered riches and counted them over, thinking his riches have made him immortal!

ISLAM: *Qur'an 104.1–3*

B E NOT content with the ease of a passing day, and deprive not thyself of everlasting rest. Barter not the garden of eternal delight for the dust-heap of a mortal world. Up from thy prison ascend unto the glorious meads above, and from thy mortal cage wing thy flight unto the paradise of the Placeless.

BAHÁ'Í FAITH: *Persian Hidden Words 39*

W ATCHFULNESS IS the path of immortality: unwatchfulness is the path of death. Those who are watchful never die: those who do not watch are already as dead.

BUDDHISM: *Dhammapada 21*

H E WHOSE mind is well trained in the ways that lead to light, who surrenders the bondage of attachments and finds joy in his freedom from bondage, who, free from the darkness of passions, shines pure in a radiance of light, even in this mortal life enjoys the immortal Nirvana.

BUDDHISM: *Dhammapada 89*

O SON OF Man! Thou art My dominion and My dominion perisheth not, wherefore fearest thou thy perishing? Thou art My light and My light shall never be extinguished, why dost thou dread extinction? Thou art My glory and My glory fadeth not; thou art My robe and My robe shall never be outworn. Abide then in thy love for Me, that thou mayest find Me in the realm of glory.

BAHÁ'Í FAITH: *Arabic Hidden Words 14*

LIFE AS PREPARATION FOR DEATH

DEATH CARRIES away the man who gathers flowers, whose mind is attached to sensuality, even as a great flood sweeps away a slumbering village.

BUDDHISM: *Dhammapada 47*

EVERY BREATH you take is a step toward death.

ISLAM: *Nahjul Balagha, Saying 72*

N IGHT HATH succeeded day, and day hath succeeded night, and the hours and moments of your lives have come and gone, and yet none of you hath, for one instant, consented to detach himself from that which perisheth. Bestir yourselves, that the brief moments that are still yours may not be dissipated and lost. Even as the swiftness of lightning your days shall pass, and your bodies shall be laid to rest beneath a canopy of dust. What can ye then achieve? How can ye atone for your past failure?

BAHÁ'Í FAITH: *Gleanings 151*

THIS WORLD is like a vestibule before the World to Come; prepare yourself in the vestibule that you may enter the hall.

JUDAISM: *Mishnah, Abot 4.21*

YELLOW LEAVES hang on your tree of life. The messengers of death are waiting. You are going to travel far away. Have you any provision for the journey?

BUDDHISM: *Dhammapada 235*

BOTH LIFE and death of such as are firm in their penance and rules are good. When alive they earn merit and when dead they attain beatitude.

Both life and death of such as indulge in sins are bad. When alive they add to malice and when dead they are hurled into darkness.

JAINISM: *Dharmadasaganin, Upadesamala*

FEW CROSS the river of time and reach Nirvana. Most of them run up and down on this side of the river.

But those who, when they know the law, follow the path of the law, shall reach the other shore and go beyond the realm of death.

BUDDHISM: *Dhammapada 85–86*

O PEOPLE! FEAR God, and whatever you do, do it anticipating death. Try to attain everlasting blessing in return for transitory and perishable wealth, power, and pleasures of this world.

Be prepared for a fast passage because here you are destined for a short stay. Always be ready for death, for you are living under its shadow. Be wise like people who have heard the message of God and have taken a warning from it . . .

You must remember to gather from this life such harvest as will be of use and help to you hereafter.

ISLAM: *Nahjul Balagha, Sermon 67*

W HOEVER HARMS another being, seeking his own happiness, will find no happiness thereafter. But whoever, seeking happiness, harms no other being will find happiness hereafter . . .

He who harms the harmless and defenseless, soon will come to no good: He will suffer pain, disaster, injury, or sickness; loss of mind, oppression, accusation; or loss of loved ones, or loss of wealth, or a ravaging fire that will burn his house. And after death, this foolish man will be reborn in hell.

BUDDHISM: *Dhammapada 131–32, 137–40*

DO NOT lay up for yourselves treasures on earth, where moth and rust consume and where thieves break in and steal, but lay up for yourselves treasure in heaven, where neither moth nor rust consumes and where thieves do not break in and steal. For where your treasure is, there will your heart be also.

CHRISTIANITY: *Matthew 6.19–21*

O SHREWD BUSINESSMAN, do only profitable business: Deal only in that commodity which shall accompany you after death.

SIKHISM: *Adi Granth, Sri Ragu M.1*

MEN WHO have not led a religious life and have not laid up the true treasures of life in their youth, perish like old herons in a lake without fish. Men who have not lived a religious life and have not laid up the true treasures of life in their youth lie like worn-out bows, sighing after the past.

BUDDHISM: *Dhammapada 155–56*

THE NEXT WORLD

YOU PREFER this life, although the life to come is better and more enduring.

ISLAM: *Qur'an 87.16–17*

THE WORLD beyond is as different from this world as this world is different from that of the child while still in the womb of its mother. When the soul attains the Presence of God, it will assume the form that best befits its immortality and is worthy of its celestial habitation.

BAHÁ'Í FAITH: *Gleanings 81*

W HEN A MAN considers this world as a bubble of froth, and as the illusion of an appearance, then the king of death has no power over him . . .

This world is indeed in darkness, and how few can see the light! Just as few birds escape from a net, so few souls can fly into the freedom of heaven.

BUDDHISM: *Dhammapada 170, 174*

N OT LIKE this world is the World to Come. In the World to Come there is neither eating nor drinking; no procreation of children or business transactions; no envy or hatred or rivalry; but the righteous sit enthroned, their crowns on their heads, and enjoy the luster of the Divine Splendor.

JUDAISM: *Talmud*

I N MY Father's house are many rooms.

CHRISTIANITY: *John 14.2*

K NOW THAT the present life is but a sport and a diversion, an adornment and a cause of boasting among you, and a rivalry in wealth and children. It is as a rain whose vegetation pleases the unbelievers, then it withers, and you see it turning yellow, then it becomes straw. And in the Hereafter there is grievous punishment, and forgiveness from God and good pleasure; whereas the present life is but the joy of delusion.

ISLAM: *Qur'an 57.20*

R ELATIVES AND friends and well-wishers rejoice at the arrival of a man who had been long absent and has returned home safely from afar. Likewise, meritorious deeds will receive the good person upon his arrival in the next world, as relatives welcome a dear one on his return.

BUDDHISM: *Dhammapada 219–20*

W HEN THE human soul soareth out of this transient heap of dust and riseth into the world of God, then veils will fall away, and verities will come to light, and all things unknown before will be made clear, and hidden truths be understood.

BAHÁ'Í FAITH: *Selections from the Writings of 'Abdu'l-Bahá*

A S FOR THAT abode of the Hereafter, We assign it to those who seek not oppression in the earth, nor corruption. The sequel is for those who ward off evil. Whoever brings a good deed, he will have better than the same; while as for him who brings an ill deed, those who do ill deeds will be requited only what they did.

ISLAM: *Qur'an 28.83–84*

H E IS HAPPY in this world and he is happy in the next world: the man who does good is happy in both worlds. He is glad, he feels great gladness when he sees the good he has done.

BUDDHISM: *Dhammapada 16*

Progress of the Soul

T HOSE WHO remember Me at the time of death will come to Me. Do not doubt this. Whatever occupies the mind at the time of death determines the destiny of the dying; always they will tend toward that state of being. Therefore, remember Me at all times.

HINDUISM: *Bhagavad Gita 8.5–7*

K NOW THOU of a truth that the soul, after its separation from the body, will continue to progress until it attaineth the presence of God, in a state and condition which neither the revolution of ages and centuries, nor the changes and chances of this world, can alter.

BAHÁ'Í FAITH: *Gleanings 79*

Toward the wicked man and the righteous one
And him in whom right and wrong meet
Shall the Judge act in upright manner,
According to the laws of the present existence.

Zoroastrianism: *Avesta, Yasna 33.1*

WHEN HE thus departs, life departs; and when life departs, all the functions of the vital principle depart. The Self remains conscious, and, conscious, the dying man goes to his abode. The deeds of this life, and the impressions they leave behind, follow him . . .

As a goldsmith, taking an old gold ornament, molds it to another, newer and more beautiful, so the Self, having given up the body and left it unconscious, takes on a newer and better form.

HINDUISM: *Brihadaranyaka Upanishad 4.4.1–4*

L o! WE have shown man the way, whether he be grateful or disbelieving.

ISLAM: *Qur'an 76.3*